HOW I SOLD

100,000

CHILDREN'S BOOKS

DAVID BLAZE

How I Sold 100,000 Children's Books

Copyright © 2020 by David Blaze

For Zander...

Wow! That's Epic!

Children's Books
by David Blaze

My Fox Ate My Homework

My Fox Ate My Cake

My Fox Ate My Alarm Clock

My Cat Ate My Homework

My Fox Begins

My Fox Ate My Report Card

My Fox, My Friend Forever

Janie Gets A Genie For Christmas

My Little Fox Says Please

Epic Kids

Gotta Catch The Easter Bunny

My Fox And Friends Word Search

My Skunk Goes To School

Table of Contents

THIS IS WHO I AM

I left my full-time job in 2018 because I was making more money with writing children's books and I wanted more time to focus on that. I had written five picture books and chapter books in a year and a half and had two more ready to go. During that time I had built many relationships with other authors.

I was on my way to Chili's one afternoon with my wife and son when she snatched my phone from me as it kept vibrating with incoming messages. She scrolled through the messages, probably checking to see if I had a side chick.

"You've got to stop this," she said. "You're helping all of them get ahead while you get nothing in return."

Three authors were messaging me at the same time for help with publishing and marketing. Dozens more would reach out to me throughout the day. It was impossible for me to ignore them. Most of my working career had been based on leading others and helping them achieve their best work.

"They need my help," I argued. "This is who I am."

"That's not who you have to be." I should have known she wouldn't accept my answer. We had been married for twelve years and she knew what was best for me because, hey, women know everything. "Tell me this: how much time do you write every day?"

"Four or five hours," I said. "The rest of it is spent making notes and advertising."

She held up a hand and said, "Wait a minute. During that time I know you're getting messages from other authors and helping them. How do you have time to write anything?"

She was right, of course. My written word output had slowed from a marathon to a limp walk. I sighed in defeat. "I like helping others. It's not fair if I know how to do something but don't share it with them when they ask. What am I supposed to do?"

She responded to all my text messages, saying that I was busy and had to go, then handed the phone back to me. "You can help other authors, but you've got to find a way to make money doing it. Otherwise, you're not writing and losing money because of it."

I hated that she was right. I had left my job to have

more time to write, but instead I was working for free for others and had less time to write.

It's two years later now and when other authors reach out to me, I answer their question then apologize and explain that I can't answer more questions because I have to focus on my writing (authors never have just one question—it's always dozens or hundreds). Just between you and me, I always end with, "Because my wife won't let me."

Anyway, I'm a writer above all else. I may create an online course one day, but for now I'm going to do what I do best. I'm going to write. I'll share with you all of my experiences in writing and how I got to where I am today. My promise to you is that I will tell you my story as if we were best friends standing face-to-face. I'll tell you my failures and my triumphs on the road to selling 100,000 children's books. I'll tell it to you this way because I want to see you succeed.

BEFORE I WAS
A CHILDREN'S AUTHOR

I didn't start out writing books for kids. No, years before that I wrote horror short stories for adults.

Back in 2003, I belonged to Francis Ford Coppola's writing site Zoetrope.com. It allows writers of all levels to post short stories and novellas to be reviewed by other writers for free (now I see it also has screenplays, short scripts, poetry, and novels. You can join on the site under Zoetrope Workshops). I just logged in for the first time in 17 years and see that I had 57 submissions and reviewed 285 stories. I had to read and review five short stories to get one of mine reviewed. The reviews aren't meant for the public to see. The sole purpose is to help writers improve their craft (that, and for Mr. Coppola to determine if he wants one of the stories to be printed in his magazine).

(I was diagnosed with multiple sclerosis in January of that year and out of work for the entire year. This allowed me to read, write, and review stories all day and all night.)

Each review gives stories a rating from 1 to 10 (1, bad

– 10, good). The first stories I posted were rated 1–3. The reviews were vicious and told me that I had no idea how to write. Because of the nature of the site, the reviews also explained how I needed to fix my stories in terms of grammar, dialogue, settings, etc. I became angry and refused to listen to them because I thought I knew everything about writing (even though I had never studied it).

After posting several stories and getting the same negative feedback, I decided to take their advice and reposted the stories to show them I had been right all along. Before I could repost them, I realized my stories were much better with the suggested changes.

The ratings were no longer 1–3. They were 4–6 and I started getting compliments. I began to listen to all the advice and reposted again later. My average score became 8.5 and after all these years I am still listed as a top 1% reviewer because I absorbed all of the advice and could pass it on to others. This was my training ground for how to write with the written and unwritten rules of grammar. It also changed me from a pantser to a plotter.

The stories I wrote were combined into a collection that was contracted with a publisher in 2006.

I wish I could say I sold a ton of copies of that book. Honestly, it only sold one copy during the entire seven years it was with a publisher. That one copy sold in the United Kingdom, which is a beautiful country, but I was ashamed because I couldn't sell a single copy in my own country (the United States).

When the contract ended in 2013, I considered self-publishing my masterpiece. It's important to know that up until that point I had seen "self-published" as a dirty word. But it was impossible to do worse than selling one copy with a "gatekeeper" (publisher).

My wife and I stopped by a local Barnes and Noble one afternoon. She searched the aisles for romance novels while I flipped through a *Writer's Digest* and came across an article about eBooks. I was shocked to find that self-published eBooks were starting to outsell paperback books. I went home that same day, formatted my book for Kindle, found a book cover designer on Fiverr.com, and published it online at kdp.amazon.com within 48 hours.

The eBook immediately started selling two copies a day every day. Financially speaking, it wasn't that great—but it was a huge ego boost. I got 35 cents for every copy sold so I basically made $21 a month. In those days, it was enough to pay for a full tank of gas, which was a blessing because my wife and I had just adopted a newborn baby we named Zander Blaze. While we both had full-time jobs, it was difficult to pay all the bills after the adoption and other medical expenses. We even had to swallow our pride and ask our parents for money.

I couldn't shake the feeling that the book could sell even more copies over the next few months, but something was missing. I had the cover redesigned four times without any change in sales volume. After the fifth redesign and a title change, I started selling four copies a day. I was beyond excited to bring home $42 a month (this was the same book that had brought me less than $2 in seven years).

Still, I knew I could sell more. I didn't know at that time that books on Amazon could be listed in ten categories if you asked the support team to place them there, so I was stuck with the standard two categories for the next three years. I changed the two categories to see if the book could pick up a larger audience. My sales got worse, so I changed them back. When sales returned to normal, I tried two more categories. The next day, I was selling 12 copies and more every day after that—$126 a month.

At that point I couldn't think of anything else to change. So I wrote a sequel. Not as many sales with that but an additional six every day. So I wrote five more sequels. By the time all the books settled, and the series was complete, I was selling 30 copies a day and averaging $300 a month. That allowed me to cover all gas and groceries for the next few years. This turned out to be a godsend because Zander Blaze had been born seven weeks early, was underweight, and required being fed every two hours. The diapers and formula added up quickly.

Three years after I started selling two copies a day that increased to 30 copies, my sales dried up and withered away. It wasn't a gradual decline in sales. They literally dropped from 30 sales a day to two sales overnight. Just like that, I was back to making $21 a month and it only got worse. Within a few months, I sold one copy some days and zero copies other days.

As my sales slipped deeper and deeper, I felt completely defeated but I couldn't stop thinking about writing a time travel fantasy for my sister. There was something I had to do first that I hadn't done since I was nine years old though.

I had to visit her grave.

FACING FEARS

It was December 2015 when Regina, Zander, and I headed to South Florida. We were familiar with the drive because our favorite vacation spots were Fort Lauderdale and Pompano Beach. My entire adult life I had wanted to return to South Florida, where I had grown up, and I never understood why. We settled on living in Orlando and heading south whenever we could.

Zander had just turned two years old and was already showing signs of being a fireball. He was a determined, persistent little boy who fought to get what he wanted (he's almost seven now and that hasn't changed). We headed to Loxahatchee first, so he could see the animals at Lion Country Safari. That may have been a mistake. We've learned through the years that he isn't a huge fan of animals.

We went to my old neighborhood in Royal Palm Beach right after. It was only a few miles outside of Loxahatchee. I hadn't seen it since moving away when I was fourteen. There was a specific spot on the road before my childhood home that I had to see, and it scared me beyond measure as we got closer. It was the spot where I had watched Sarah die.

One thing that has frustrated me for most of my life is that I have no memory of my childhood. None before December 17th, 1986 when I was nine and Sarah was seven. What happened that day is the first memory of my life that I have.

I won't go into deep details, and you can skip the rest of this chapter if you need to. I'm only sharing it because it explains why I wrote the way I used to and why I write the way I do now.

It was eight days before Christmas, and Sarah was hit by a speeding van when riding her bike through the intersection our street was on. I was behind her.

A year and a half later, when I started middle school, I had to ride the bus because the school was a ways out. The bus stop I waited at every day for three and a half years was at the exact spot where Sarah died. There was no way to ignore it. A large stain had been left on the road.

As Regina, Zander, and I got closer to that spot, I held my breath. I'm not sure how to explain it, but I knew that if the spot was gone then I would be free.

It was gone!

Overwhelming relief, but there was still one more thing I had to do. We headed to the cemetery.

The grass in the cemetery was tall. I watched as Zander waded through it while Regina led him. I thought it would be easy to find the grave because we had stopped by the front office and got a map with the exact location, but we had to split up to find it. The number of graves was massive.

Regina found it first and called me over as she pulled Zander away to give me time to do whatever I needed to do. I didn't tell her my purpose for being there and she never asked. She knew it was important to me and that's all that mattered to her.

I stood before the grave and made Sarah a promise I should have made years before.

When we drove away and past Royal Palm Beach, I whispered, "Goodbye." I had wanted to return there to live, but now the desire was gone.

I suppose it's only fitting that my horror collection stopped selling completely after that day.

The time travel story for Sarah hasn't been written

yet. My friend Erick asked me why one night. I told him I won't write it until I'm the best writer I can be. I owe it to her. I'll keep writing, keep publishing, keep getting better, and I'll know when the time is right.

If you have something in your past that's keeping you from moving ahead, maybe it's time to face it. It doesn't matter whether it's from your childhood or it happened yesterday, there's no reason for it to keep you from reaching your dreams.

MY FIRST CHILDREN'S BOOK

When Zander was younger, my wife and I were concerned because he didn't move much for the first seven months. Near the end of month eight, he started crawling nonstop. That's when we realized he was persistent, or as my wife likes to say, "stubborn". Zander didn't want to crawl—he wanted to walk—and he kept trying to over and over again. He couldn't do it, of course, because he hadn't perfected crawling yet. He got upset every time he fell down and threw whatever objects were around him.

But he kept trying.

Two weeks later, he was walking and standing on top of tables like the king of a mountain.

Zander's persistence in everything he does inspired me in the summer of 2016. I realized that I couldn't give up on my writing—it had been a part of me since I was a kid. I sat down and drafted as many story ideas as I could. I believe there were fourteen of them. Thirteen were horror, just like I had written in the past. But the fourteenth one was different, and I couldn't stop thinking about it.

It was something like this: "Boy meets a fox in the woods and makes it his pet because his mom won't let him get a dog."

Over the next few days I crossed out my story ideas one by one until I could decide what to write. I was shocked to find the boy and fox standing alone after all the other ideas were tossed aside. It would have been easy to make that a horror story, but something didn't feel right about that. I had dabbled in fantasy before and wondered how I could fit the boy and fox into a fantasy world.

I struggled with this for days but then asked myself, "What can the fox do that other foxes can't do?" And then it hit me. "What if the fox is a kid (kit) and can talk?" Okay, that could be interesting. "What would the fox say to the boy when they first met?"

As a side note, whenever I have an idea for a new story now, I always start with the question "What if?" Let's say I wanted to write a story about a blade of grass that's shorter than all the other blades around it. I know, lame example, but listen. What if that blade knows it's shorter than the others? What if every time the wind blows the other blades laugh and dance around him (or her)? What if that blade is a different color? What if that blade eventually grows taller than the others? What if the grass is cut and then they're all the same size?

There are many directions this story could go. I don't claim any rights to the idea so feel free to make a masterpiece about a short blade of grass.

As for the boy and fox, I realized it wasn't right for me to put them in a fantasy world. I wanted them to be in the real world with the fantasy element of talking animals. That's not an original idea so I had to do more.

That's when my "what if" came into play. "What if the fox can talk because the forest gave him that power? What if his eyes turned blue because of it? What if that power extends to the boy in another form?" Now I was getting excited.

I knew at that point that the story had to be for children. There was one problem though. I had no idea how to write for children!

Over the next month I read as many children's books as I could. I read picture books, chapter books, and middle grade novels. I was shocked to find that I enjoyed chapter books and middle grade novels (my bookshelf had always been full of Stephen King and Dan Brown books). The new fascination I had with books for younger audiences turned out to be important. I've come to believe you can't write an amazing book unless you read and enjoy the same type of writing.

I was ready. The next challenge for me was time. I worked full time in a call center and had a wife and child at home. I was used to writing short stories in my spare time, but this new idea required much more time, mainly because I couldn't get it out of my head, no matter how much the story progressed. It began to feel like torture when I couldn't write.

I took a shift working 3:00 p.m. till midnight, allowing me to write before and after work. I got home roughly ten minutes after midnight and stayed up for the next four hours, writing as much as I could. Now, I'm not a fast writer. I consistently write 500 words an hour, which I'm the most comfortable with.

My job being so close, I had another two hours or more to write after I woke up. If you're calculating the time and 500 words an hour, you may think I was pounding out 3000 words or more a day. That book turned out to be 18,000 words so six days should have been enough.

I wish.

The story went through dozens of revisions because, hey, even though I had just read tons of children's books, I was wandering around a whole new universe. What I wrote wasn't enough; something was still missing. Back to "what if?" What if the boy just moved to a new home and starts at a new school? What if he's bullied at school? What if the new home is in the country and he's from the city? What if his uncle is a hunter? What if his uncle hunts foxes?

Three months later, I had a draft I was happy with. I sent it to three beta readers I found on Fiverr to see if they had any ideas on how to improve it. Now, there's a general consensus with authors that beta readers should not be paid. I agree if the sole purpose is to find out if they like the story or not, but I use them for much more than that.

Zoetrope taught me the value of beta readers. It taught me how vicious strangers who know the craft can be. It taught me that I want my beta readers to be vicious with detailed explanations. For that, and if they have a proven record, I am willing to pay a premium.

So I sent my new book with the fox to three beta readers. I've come to believe that if one beta tells me there's a problem, they could be right. If two betas tell me the same thing, they're probably right. If all three tell me the same problem(s), then I've got work to do. They suggested numerous changes and I made most of them.

For the first time, I decided to use a line editor (I always use one now). I used the cheapest editor I could find ($5 on Fiverr). She found and corrected numerous grammar errors, which I was grateful for. A year after publication I found a few more. Unwilling to risk more unknown errors, I paid a new editor hundreds of dollars, and the cleaner version is impeccable.

I decided to self-publish the book I named *My Fox Ate My Homework* on CreateSpace as a paperback in November 2016. Amazon bought CreateSpace some time back and merged the systems a couple of years ago, making it all Kindle Direct Publishing (KDP). I also put the book up as a Kindle eBook.

I had a ton of confidence that this book would do awesomely well and far surpass my former horror collection. I had never put so much emotion and work into one piece of writing. The book was going to be a huge hit, selling thousands.

First month combined sales: 43

I felt sick.

SOCIAL MEDIA SITES
AND ADVERTISING

For years I tried to convince my wife that when I consistently made $1,000 a month from my books, I needed to leave my full-time job and work somewhere part time. This was so I would have three or four more hours a day to write, potentially matching the income I made working full time. After that I could leave the part-time job to write full time.

I surpassed $1,000 a month four months after *My Fox Ate My Homework* was released.

I never took a part-time job, even though my sales and income increased every month. There were two reasons for this. One was I loved my job and the people I worked with. The other was I made a new plan to prove I could make a full-time income with my books for a full year before I left my job.

The day after my book was released, I set out to put myself on as many social media platforms as I was comfortable with. I was already familiar with my personal page on Facebook, so I created a business page with my author name. You can still find me there as David Blaze, Children's Author if you'd like to see what I've done. The page has collected more than 10,000 followers over the years.

I created an Author Central account for Amazon on authorcentral.amazon.com so I could claim my book, post my author picture to my book sales page, and write a short biography for all readers to see. I also used it to upload a video to my sales page that promoted the book. The video was created on Fiverr.com. You can find it on the *My Fox Ate My Homework* page on Amazon near the bottom, where it says: Videos for this product.

I also created an author profile on Goodreads and uploaded my book cover and information there. I've never used the site much, but I've read over the years that it's a popular place for readers to find and discuss books. I uploaded my video there as well.

I created a YouTube channel and had a handful of videos about the book made for that. Most are humorous. One is a spat between puppets. Several teachers read a few chapters of the book aloud for their students there (with my permission). You can find all of those on YouTube by searching for ... drumroll ... My Fox Ate My Homework.

I created a Pinterest page to post my one book on (now it has all of them). I had never used Pinterest, but many people I worked with talked about how they found recipes and crafts on there. They explained the whole site was based on pictures. I thought, *Hey, my book cover is a picture, so why not post it?*

I created a LinkedIn profile to announce I was a children's author. No one knew who I was, and I wasn't even sure I was really a children's author, but I remembered something I'd heard years before, loosely: Write your resume for the job you want, not the job you have. There wasn't much to put on there yet and I doubted anyone would ever see it. I uploaded my profile picture and information about my book, plus a way to contact me. I never thought that doing that would change my life one day (more information later).

I created an author website using Godaddy.com and, of course, I uploaded the video there. Again, I didn't expect anything to happen with that. The site typically gets 600–2000 views a month. Many amazing things have happened with it. I've been contacted by kids, parents, schools, an agent, and publishers through the site. You can view it here:

DavidBlazeBooks.com

I paid for three Readers' Favorite reviews. You don't have to pay—they will consider one review for free. The reviews can't be added to the customer reviews on Amazon per rules, but you are allowed to place them in Editorial Reviews. You do this from Author Central. I paid for the reviews because I recognized the value of social proof. If your book doesn't have any reviews, it's hard to convince readers to buy it. The simple psychology is that if X number of people like a book, then you may like it too. It's been touted over the years that your book should have twenty reviews to convince a larger number of readers to buy it. I'm not sure that's true. If you can get at least three reviews as soon as possible, your chances of greater sales are much better than with a lingering zero. You can find out more about Readers' Favorite at readersfavorite.com. (P.S. I won the 2020 Gold Medal award in the Preteen category from them this month! The book is *Epic Kids*.)

I paid for images on Depositphotos.com. Chapter books for an age range of 8–12 generally (not always) do best with spot illustrations. In terms of the age range, if you list it as 7–10 or 8–12, some five, six, and seven-year-olds will read it because kids like to read 'up'. The images I used are digital, and that sometimes gets complaints from adults. I have at least three reviews from adults (even a teacher) complaining about it. They usually give the book a 1-star rating, even though the same reviews also state their kids loved it. The reason I didn't use an illustrator in the early days was because I didn't have the money for it. I've decided not to swap out the digital images because I've grown to love them.

I did all of this within three days after the book was released. There are other social platforms like Instagram and Twitter, but I opted not to use those because I don't want to juggle a billion swords at once. I picked what I was comfortable and somewhat familiar with. I encourage you to pick at least two social media sites to post information about your book on. You never know who's watching but chances are that at some point someone with the right power, connections, advice, etc. will come along to help you get to where you want to be.

The other thing I did that really helped was I joined a few author groups on Facebook. Many of these groups have writers at all levels who willingly share their experiences in writing, publishing, marketing and even advertising. I was a lurker for more than a year because I didn't have any advice to offer yet. I learned a ton by reading new posts and older posts. I don't know about you, but I'm not a hands-on learner. I've excelled at every job that allows me to learn by reading.

This led me to learning about something called Amazon Marketing Services (or AMS). It has since been renamed Amazon Advertising, but most authors still call it AMS. You need to understand that I never wanted to do any advertising. I hated the idea of spending money to maybe make money. I had grown up hearing, "You have to spend money to make money," all the time. I assumed that was something only rich people did.

I spent $5 the first day because I figured it wouldn't be a huge loss. I set up one manual ad and one automatic. The manual ads require you to put in keywords you think readers will search for when they are on Amazon. Those keywords often show the product you are advertising. I decided to use author names and book titles that seemed similar to mine. The automatic ad was simply Amazon deciding which words were best. I was awed to find out the next day that I would be getting $15 back from sales reached though advertising. Ten dollars profit equaled 200% more than my $5 investment. I was hooked!

I tried Facebook ads then and I still do sometimes today. I've taken online courses and read several books about them. It hasn't worked out for my books. The profit, if there is any, is rarely more than 5%. Don't get me wrong; I've seen evidence that some authors are successful with this. In fact, they are so successful that they sell many more books than I do.

I ordered a PayPal credit card reader for my phone. Most people don't carry around cash anymore and I wanted to be ready if someone I knew wanted to buy the book from me. I think the reader was free. PayPal charges something like 2% or 3% of every transaction; I figured losing 3% of $5 or $10 is painless compared to gaining 100% of zero dollars if all someone had was a debit or credit card.

Anyway, after publishing my book and taking care of the above social media and ads, I was exhausted. I had spent months getting four or five hours of sleep. You have to remember that I have multiple sclerosis. Any time I get less than eight hours of sleep, my body doesn't work right. Typically it gives me major balance issues. I learned how to mask it over the years and lean or press against walls, tables, and desks without drawing attention.

I took my book to work with me soon after and placed it on my desk for everyone to see. The cover was beautiful and shiny. There's a rumor that authors are conceited. I'm not sure why we would ever be that way just because we have big imaginations and can put those thoughts into written words. I think most of us have a "Look at me! Look at me!" complex. We just want the world to see us and accept us.

A good friend and co-worker of mine named Suzanne stopped by my desk. She congratulated me and thumbed through a few pages. What she said next set me on the path to reaching my goals.

REQUIRED SACRIFICE

It was late November 2016 and hotter than the inside of a broken refrigerator in Orlando. Suzanne and I had started working together at the call center on the same day almost exactly three years earlier. She had been promoted twice and was a trainer. She asked me if I was ready to write another book.

I was still exhausted from all the work I had put into *My Fox Ate My Homework* and couldn't imagine doing it again and losing so much sleep. Plus, early signs showed that the book would not be a big success. I had no intention of writing another children's book. I told her as much.

"Is this what you want to do with your life?" she asked, holding up my book.

I told her yes because writing stories and books full time is what I had always wanted to do. I also told her that it had left me drained and had taken all of my free time. I had missed so much sleep that I wasn't even sure what day it was.

"If you have to sacrifice sleep for two or three years so you can live the rest of your life the way you want it to be, then that's what you should do."

I fought with the idea but realized she was right (remember, women are always right). I asked myself the "what if" questions normally reserved for my characters. What if I could live my dream of writing full time within two or three years? What if the sacrifice I had to make was sleep? I had read before that to achieve something great you have to sacrifice something else—usually hobbies, TV shows, or even relationships. If you think about it, all of these relate to time.

I decided to make that sacrifice (sleep). It affected my family because I had less time to spend with them. I lived with the belief it would be short term. I knew that if I could accomplish my goal within a few years then I would have more time than ever to spend with them. I'd be able to go to any school events with Zander. I'd be home with him during holidays and vacations from school. I'd always be available to take care of him if he got sick.

Another friend and co-worker of mine named Syreeta was the first person to swipe a card for the book. She started working at the call center soon after I was promoted to an operations lead. I learned a lot from her over the years.

Syreeta was also a hair stylist who owned her own company and took more vacations than anyone else I knew at the time. She strongly believed in a work and play balance. She found ways to improve her knowledge of business by constantly reading books and attending conferences that gave her the tools to be the best.

I began to read tons of books on business and growth mindsets. I became a fan of success books by Napoleon Hill and Jack Canfield. There are many other leaders that have much to teach about success principles. I would encourage you to read some of these books or even attend some of their conferences. I can honestly say it put me in a mindset that I was capable of achieving what seemed impossible at the time.

And then there was Erick. He worked the overnight shift and we crossed paths often before my shift ended. I hung out at his desk talking about dumb guy things like nunchucks for at least thirty minutes on nights we both worked. I'm mostly a serious guy who likes to be silly sometimes. Erick is … well … he's Erick.

He became more and more involved with making YouTube videos (and still does). The first one I saw was from before I met him when he lighted a fart on fire. I believe it was his most viewed video at the time. He took on a fascination with drones, filming beaches and parks from high in the sky. He also reviewed camping equipment and boating gear.

Soon companies were sending him products to review on his channel. I watched his excitement as he gained more and more followers. He showed me the ins and out of creating videos on YouTube and how to monetize them. I'm fairly sure he'll be famous one day.

Erick became the second half of my brain trust. I explained my advertising on Amazon and he explained his advertising on YouTube. We traded ideas that helped open doors to things we couldn't see before. We even exchanged different workout plans that worked for us because, hey, that's what bros do.

As authors and writers, 99% of our work is done alone. I shut myself in my office with my dog and take off my hearing aids to block out the world (oh yeah, I wear hearing aids). But we really need an outside source to help us see things from another angle. I'd encourage you to find someone like you who can help you accomplish more with just a little insight into things you never considered. We live in a digital world, so it doesn't have to be in person.

BETA READERS AND EDITORS

As Christmas passed and the new year began in 2017, I decided to make a sequel to *My Fox Ate My Homework*. I had read many posts in Facebook author groups that suggested series books sell better than standalone books. I remembered that when I created sequels for my horror collection, my overall sales more than doubled, and so did my income.

The second book took me two months to write and revise. I named it *My Fox Ate My Cake*. Like the first one, it was just over 100 pages. I was leery to write my books this short because books like Harry Potter, which are for the same age range, are over 300 pages.

When I was younger, I read a ton of books because I loved to read. I remember reading books of all lengths and enjoying them for different reasons. The most exciting ones to me were the ones around 100 pages because the action moved faster and made me excited to race to the next chapter. I think that's what I was trying to accomplish with this series.

Based on reviews and feedback I've received over the years, I have a large audience with reluctant readers. These are the kids that don't love to read books and would rather give an angry cat a bubble bath. Many of these kids get hooked on this series and keep reading until it's complete. Will I write a 300-page book one day? Yeah, probably, but not in this series.

Like before, I sent my final draft to three beta readers and made the necessary updates before sending it to an editor. There's another contention with authors about when a book should go to beta readers. Technically, betas are supposed to see the final product, which many would interpret to mean written, edited, and formatted so they can make overall suggestions. My problem with this logic is that if the beta reader(s) suggests major changes and you implement them, it would likely need to go back to an editor again. I'm not willing to risk paying hundreds of dollars twice for the same book.

You may have noticed earlier that I use Fiverr for many things book related. I'm sure there are varying opinions about this, and that's fine. Always use the resources that are best for you. My beta readers, cover designers, editor, and video producers all come from Fiverr. The sellers are rated and reviewed by buyers so there is plenty of social proof for what works and what doesn't. Plus, you see examples of the most recent work they have done. No, not everything there is $5. I spend an average of $1,050 a year on Fiverr.

I don't want these numbers to scare you. I typically write three books a year and the above expenses are based on that. You don't have to have a cover designer if you can create covers yourself. At the same time, you can buy premade covers with a simple search on Google, and the artists will modify the title and name for you. You can use sites like Reedsy.com where there are award-winning artists, but they are pricey. Places like Fiverr and Reedsy also have illustrators if you want to hire one for you book. There are programs like Canva that you can design covers on for free. I don't have any art ability, never have, and will always outsource it to professionals.

Beta readers are a good idea, but you shouldn't use your family or friends. It's hard, nearly impossible, for them to be impartial, whether they mean to be or not. Maybe they loved you last week but you did something this week that ticked them off and they're eagerly digging your grave. Always use strangers. If you can't pay for them or think it's silly to do that, have a friend's friends read your work, or better yet, have your neighbors' kids read it. The downside to doing it this way is they are not professionals that have reviewed dozens or hundreds of works and aren't likely to make in-dept suggestions. Another thing you can do instead is hire a developmental editor (I've done this before), which is like a beta reader on steroids.

I highly recommend paying for a line/copy editor unless you're best friends with a college English professor. They will correct all of your grammar and improve it. I've gone over some of my earlier work (not published) and find new errors every time. That's what happened with *My Fox Ate My Homework* when I looked over it a year later, even though it had been edited. My advice based on that— don't pay $5 for an editor. The standard advice if you can't afford a good editor is to put your manuscript in a drawer for three months and leave it there. When you take it out three months later, you'll have fresh eyes and see things you didn't notice before, guaranteed (I did this in the old days). There are also books like *Self-Editing for Fiction Writers* that are popular.

Don't stress about the potential upfront expenses. Depending on your talents and how much you're willing to learn, it could cost you exactly $0 to publish your book. I decided years ago to outsource all work that is not related to writing my books (with the exception of advertising). This puts less stress on me and gives me more time and energy to focus on what I do best.

I put the *My Fox Ate My Cake* eBook on pre-order on Amazon three weeks before its release in April 2017. I released the paperback five days before the eBook was live. There's a reason for that.

I had released the eBook and paperback versions of My Fox Ate My Homework on the same day. I quickly noticed something about the sales page where all versions of the book are listed (paperback, eBook, hardcover, audio); there wasn't just one sales page, there were two—one for the paperback and one for the eBook. It took five days before they were combined. I always stagger releases now so both versions release on the same day or at least close together. Amazon says it can take up to ten days for versions to combine, and, yes, this has happened to me before.

The *My Fox Ate My Cake* eBook had seventeen pre-orders. Not great but I wasn't sweating yet. I started to see a pattern with the paperback versions of the books. Seventy percent of my sales were paperback and thirty percent were eBook. This went against everything I had learned in the Facebook groups where it was touted that all focus needed to be on the eBooks because they sold the most. I later joined children's author groups because I had not been in groups focused on children's books and found they mostly had similar patterns to mine.

For us, when creating books for early readers, chapter books, and middle grade novels, it's wise to have a paperback version. Not all of us have the same experiences, but most of us far outsell eBooks with paperbacks.

PRICES AND PROFITS

My next book in the series was released five months later in September 2017. I called that one *My Fox Ate My Alarm Clock*. At that point it was clear that it took me an average of five months to release a book. It started to worry me because many authors strive to release one book a month, or what they call a rapid release. There's a lot of evidence that if you release a book every thirty days, and the books are in a series, readers will devour them. The next eBook will already be waiting on pre-order while readers are consuming the current book. I have no doubt it's much easier to hook readers with the bait in front of them instead of casting a line the next season.

By this time my sales had increased substantially to around 1000 copies a month (700 paperbacks, 300 eBooks), but for the first time since I released *My Fox Ate My Homework* my sales dropped instead of increasing. I figured I had reached the ceiling but learned over the years that wasn't the case. There turned out to be different sales patterns with different seasons.

For me, late summer is when my sales decline for a couple of months—always August and September. I don't have a heart attack anymore because I'm prepared for it. I keep a specific savings account to cover any losses during those months and to cover extra advertising costs in December (sales increase substantially in December—the more I advertise the more I make).

Let's talk about different prices for books and advertising expenses for a minute.

When I released the first book in the series, I priced it at $6.99. I did this because most of the other books in my categories (chapter books, intermediate readers) were priced that way. After a couple of months I raised the price to $7.99. My sales still increased. A month later, I raised it again to $8.99. Believe it or not, sales kept going up. Next month, $9.99. My sales didn't slow until I hit $10.99 and I brought in less money. I reduced it back to $9.99 and kept the price there.

So that's where it stayed until November. I figured that with the holidays approaching, it would be worth a shot to increase the price because shoppers are willing to pay more. Maybe I was greedy, but I priced it at $11.99.

The $11.99 price showed on the Amazon page, but it had a slash through it. The $9.99 still showed as the actual price. I was livid with Amazon! In my misunderstanding at the time, I thought they were showing readers what the suggested price was but would still pay me for the lower $9.99 price. The fact is they were selling the book to customers for $9.99 but giving me the royalty rate for $11.99. Score!

I modify book prices throughout the year with this knowledge. I've found that if I raise a price after it's been at a lower price for only a few months, the higher slashed price won't stay very long—maybe weeks. If I leave a price low for a full year then raise it, the slashed price stays in effect for about a year.

For the first two years that my books were released, I spent an average of $500 a month on AMS (Amazon Advertising now). I once explained this to Erick and he thought I was crazy. I tried to explain the returns percentage to him, but he shook his head and said that was way too much.

I said to him, "If I give you five hundred dollars and you give me back four thousand, who wins?" His face lit up and he no longer thought $500 was too much to spend.

I won't lie to you—advertising prices have gone up in the past two years. I usually pay $700–$1000 a month for the same returns as before. You don't have to pay anywhere near that much. Four years ago, I wouldn't have been able to.

We don't get paid for the sales made this month until two months after the last day of it. It can be tough to wait that long at first because you would have to pay for advertising this month, next month, and the month after before you got paid for just this month. After that you get paid monthly. It's kind of like the old days with jobs when they held your check for the first month. I don't think most authors pay anything close to $1k at first, mostly because Amazon doesn't spend it.

Going back to *My Fox Ate My Alarm Clock*, I thought and meant for it to be the last book in the series. I felt like I had told the whole story the best way I could. I was making an income equal to my job so it was safe to try something else. I gave that story a definite ending, with Fox losing his ability to talk or even recognize the boy anymore. He returned to the forest with his parents.

In the very last sentence of that book, a stray cat

stands up and says, "Foxes can't talk." Five months later, he appeared in his own spinoff book. But first, I had another book idea I wanted to publish within two months, before Christmas.

Challenge accepted.

Remember that the first three books took five months each from first word to published. I was determined to write a Christmas story to reach a new market. I knew what I wanted to write, but I feared it wouldn't be accepted.

Janie Gets a Genie for Christmas is about a girl who finds a golden tea kettle in a gift shop. The genie inside is a boy who gives her three wishes but doesn't grant them. The things she wishes for are selfish and he convinces her to wish for things that will help other people.

The book was released on November 6, 2017. Sales were poor, as I thought they might be. Janie is a large girl and comes from a low-income family. The images depict her as such. You can call me stubborn, like Zander, but I presented Janie the way I saw her in my mind. I accepted that the book could be a complete flop.

Ten days later, on November 16, I received an email from someone claiming to be an editor for Disney Publishing Worldwide. This person asked me if I wanted to write for them.

INCREASING VISIBILITY
AND LEAVING MY JOB

Heather was the supposed editor's name. She claimed to have read *Janie Gets a Genie for Christmas* and found it a lot of fun. I didn't believe the email was real and nearly trashed it. I mean I get three fake emails a day about my Netflix account closing and passwords needing to be changed. They're pretty easy to verify just by the spelling in the emails—anywhere from one to five words are always spelled wrong.

The email from the editor passed my spelling test. But just to rule everything out, I followed the IP address, tracked down the LinkedIn profile, and found what I could on Google about this person.

By the time I was done, there was no question about it—she was the real deal.

I waited until Regina came home from work and showed her the email. Even then, I asked her if she thought it was real. She did, so I followed up with the editor.

Heather turned out to be an extraordinarily nice person. She explained that she wanted to consider me for working on novelizations with the company. I found that interesting because it was something I had never done. Admittedly, I was still leery about this being fake. I asked her how she found me. She said she found me on LinkedIn then followed it to my website. The website links to my books.

I won't go into details about the process, but after sending her the requested information to be reviewed, I didn't hear much for a full year.

Meanwhile, as 2018 came and progressed, I began to work on *My Cat Ate My Homework*. This one turned out to be challenging for me because my mind kept returning to the fox. No matter how hard I tried, I couldn't walk away from him.

At the same time I had been writing the book, I wanted to do more with *My Fox Ate My Homework*. I wondered if an audiobook would be successful with it. My concern was that I'd spend a ton of money and lose it all. I asked Erick and Syreeta if they thought it was a good idea. Both of them urged me to have it done.

I began research on ACX.com (Audible) and decided to go for it (findawayvoices.com is another popular one with authors). I don't have the kind of voice that can talk for hours; in fact, I'm a quiet guy. I set out to find a narrator on the site.

The first thing I had to do was decide on the type of contract to offer the narrators. I didn't like the idea of splitting 50% of profits with a narrator because, based on the sales of the paperback and eBook, I suspected a lot of money could be made with the audiobook. I stayed away from the royalty share, even though I wouldn't have to pay anything up front with that. I offered $200 to narrators, knowing it was on the low side, but that's what negotiations are for.

Fourteen narrators sent me samples of reading part of my book. Some were good, some were really good, and a few obviously never had voice lessons or at least the voice control needed for public speaking. I get it, they were doing what they could to make money.

Two narrators stood out to me for this project. One was a man with a gentle, friendly country accent and the other was a woman who had the voice of a Disney princess. Only one was right for this because my stories are written in first person and that person is a male.

Zachary agreed to the contract and we were off! In March 2018, the audiobook was done and live on Audible and Amazon. I turned out to be right about high sales of the book. While it's not as much as the other versions of the book, it provides a welcome addition to my profits. Honestly, I may try findawayvoices soon because they distribute to many other retailers and libraries.

In the nature of increasing the visibility of my books even more, I considered "going wide" with my eBooks in the summer of 2018. You probably know what that means, but just in case you don't, it means you take your book out of Kindle Unlimited so it's not exclusive to Amazon and make it available through other retailers. One of the most efficient ways to do this is to use an aggregator like Draft2Digital or Smashwords that can make the eBook available pretty much everywhere.

The reason I considered doing this was because I was getting an average of 30,000 KU page reads a month and felt like it was way too low. The majority of children's authors in Facebook groups seemed to face the same "problem". You never know for sure if something's going to work out better unless you try.

So, I took my books out of KU and went with Draft2Digital. It was fairly easy to upload books there and select retailers. I left them there for a few months and got very little traction. In comparison to what I had been making in KU, it was kibble. I begged Amazon to let me back in.

The strangest thing happened right after that. I got 200,000 page reads the next month. It's now two years later and I haven't gotten less than 200,000 page reads a month since. I've gotten 300,000 and 400,000 and 500,000.

I can't verify what happened to create this change, but in the two years before I tried to go wide, I didn't average more than 30k pages each month. My page reads shot up the day after I left Draft2Digital and returned to KU. Take from it what you will.

This was also the month I left my job. I'll always remember that date as well as I remember my birthday: March 17, 2018. I had told co-workers a year and a half earlier that I would be leaving to write books full time within two years. I didn't say it for them—I said it for me, putting myself on notice. Most of them were encouraging but a few were like, "Yeah, right," and laughed as if it were impossible to accomplish that.

When the time came, I put in a three-week notice. I know the standard is two, but I didn't want to leave the company in the lurch without time to find a replacement. You should've seen the look on people's faces. They were awed and shocked, like, "OMG, he really did it."

The director was at my desk every day of that three weeks, asking what the company had to do to get me to stay—all I had to do was ask. Of course I considered it for three seconds, but it's logical never to accept such an offer if you have something else to achieve. Even on my final day, right before I walked to the HR office for an exit interview, he tried to stop me and asked me to stay for at least three more months.

Stick to your guns, no matter how hard it is to walk away. I would've worked there for the rest of my life because I loved the job, but I love writing more than that. I couldn't find enough time to do all of the writing I wanted to do while holding down a job. I couldn't focus 100% on my job because I was always thinking about the next scene or another character.

Erick had a different opinion that he gave me the year before. I considered it, but it wasn't part of my dream. He said that I should keep working for the next ten years and save all the money I made from writing books. I knew that was great advice because by the end of ten years I'd have at least half a million dollars in savings, and probably much more. However, ten more years of little sleep isn't good for anyone.

So many things to think about before you leave your job. Don't be hasty. Have a clear head. I planned the finances and my production schedule for more than a year before I left. I knew the seasons when my book sales would be high and when they would be low, so the risk of unexpected surprises would be minimal.

Live your dream, but always put your family first.

My Cat Ate My Homework was released a month later, marking the return of Fox.

ISBNs AND INGRAMSPARK

Regina tried to convince me for months that I needed to write a picture book for Zander, something that he would remember forever. It was the summer of 2018 and I finally agreed with her. Zander would start VPK a few months later and he was already reading.

I decided to write a simple book about manners. Zander was familiar with my books and knew I had a fascination with foxes. What could be better than little foxes that have manners?

I created scenarios where a little fox has to say, "Please," to get what he wants. That was fairly easy for a book with 24 pages and less than 300 words. But you know how I am with art—no skills.

I vetted several illustrators on Fiverr, but it took time to find one I was comfortable with. I had him illustrate every page and scenario, and it wasn't cheap. He also made the cover. *I'm doing this for Zander, I'm doing this for Zander,* I kept repeating to myself.

When I uploaded the Kindle version of *My Little Fox Says Please*, I used a program called Kindle Kids' Book Creator that's free to download on KDP. It allows you to match illustrations with text and do pop-ups.

Once that was done, I came across my next challenge—figuring out how to put the book in hardcover. It turned out to be much easier than I thought. I had to get an ISBN first, which I did from Bowker Identifier Services. There is a charge for this, but it's much cheaper if you buy a bunch of ISBNs at once than buy one at a time.

Once I had an ISBN and the information about my book uploaded (now called *My Little Fox Says Please*), I went to IngramSpark.com and created the hardcover book there—you can't do it on Amazon. It's straightforward with a few differences from Amazon. You can set a discount for retailers that can be as low as 30% to as high as 55% and even make books returnable. Physical bookstores generally want a 55% discount and for books to be returnable. You can set the prices differently for each country.

The cool thing about using IngramSpark is that they're connected to Ingram and they are the world's largest wholesale book distributor. Your book will be available to order everywhere. Libraries and bookstores use this.

Going through this whole process, I used the other ISBNs I purchased for my other published paperback books. The reason I did this is because when purchasing ISBNs you can set an imprint name for the books. On sites like Amazon, the imprint name shows as the publisher name, making you appear as a big-name fancy publisher. I have two imprints I currently use; one is David Blaze Books and the other is Blaze Books for Young Readers. That way, on Amazon, the publisher doesn't show as Independently Published, which may unjustly turn some readers away. The book you're reading right now probably shows as Independently Published (I may change it) because it lines up with the self-published idea.

Once the new ISBNs were active, I reuploaded my paperback books on Amazon with those ISBNs instead of the Amazon-assigned ones. Once the "new books" were active, I unpublished the old books. All of the reviews automatically transferred to the new ISBNs.

I also uploaded all of my paperback books to IngramSpark so they would have wider distribution to libraries, schools, and bookstores. Yes, Amazon has its own Expanded Distribution, but you have to choose one or the other. If going through IngramSpark, you'll likely find Expanded Distribution is not available through Amazon. After two years of using IngramSpark, I'm undecided if one is better than the other. I had many sales with Expanded Distribution, but as I get older and my memory fades, I'm not sure if they were more than IS, but I believe they were. Regardless, it also adds a healthy addition to my sales and profit.

When I finally I had a physical copy of *My Little Fox Says Please* in my hands, I fell in love with it. Zander memorized the book and we often quizzed him on it. "What does My Little Fox say when he wants a snack?"

"Please!"

You get the idea. The next month Zander's VPK class and the whole daycare wanted me to do a visit and a reading. Of course I did it. I had purchased a full-body fox costume and it was time to break the bad boy out. The thing looked awesome, but the problem was it completely blocked my mouth. I asked Regina if she'd wear it so I could speak to the kids, but I guess she's claustrophobic.

She read the book to all the kids and I acted out the scenes. It was awesome for the four and five-year-olds but when we did the same thing with two and three-year-olds, they seemed lost. They had no interest in the towering fox and a couple seemed to be scared of it.

Zander loved it and that was the most important thing. He'll probably remember it for the rest of his life.

The next month and the month after, *My Little Fox Says Please* won an All-Star Bonus from Amazon for being a top 100 most read illustrated book.

I also released *My Fox Begins* at this point, a prequel to the My Fox series. It was symbolic of a new beginning for me.

AUDIBLE AND BILLBOARDS

In September 2018, I brainstormed more ways to advertise my books. My family was living in a townhouse at that time and there was a two-lane road not too far front of us. On that road and within view was a billboard that often changed advertisements, presumably because it didn't get a ton of traffic. One time there was an advertisement with James Patterson holding one of his books. I thought it was odd because I had never seen an author advertise on billboards. That advertisement disappeared within a week.

Around that same time, James Patterson had a commercial on TV promoting his books. I also thought that was odd because I hadn't seen other authors do it. The commercial was gone within weeks.

If the best-selling and highest-paid author in the world (switches between him and Rowling) was doing those things, then why couldn't I? I quickly found out why when I researched the prices for billboards and commercials!

Thanks to the power of Google, I found another

option with billboards though. There was something called blip billboards and I recognized what they were. Living in Orlando, especially when going down International Drive, there are plenty of billboards with blips. Unlike standard billboards, these are digital and change advertisements every ten seconds or so.

Using blipbillboards.com, I found that I could show an ad on hundreds of billboards throughout the United States (also Canada). Well, I could if I had a ton of money. I'll explain the process, but I ended up showing ads in eight major cities at the busiest intersections.

If you're familiar with creating ads on social sites like Amazon or Facebook, this is somewhat similar. You pay for impressions and set a daily budget. The really cool thing (to me) is you can set the exact time windows your ad shows, like between 3:00 p.m. and 6:00 p.m. This is valuable if you're placing an ad on a billboard near a school. Yes, the site shows you pictures of exact locations and even gives you traffic information based on Department of Transportation records.

The ad is an image of My Fox next to books, with

my author name on one side and the title MY FOX ATE MY HOMEWORK enlarged on the other. Beneath the fox is a banner that displays DavidBlazeBooks.com. It was $50 to have the company create it, but you can do it yourself if you're familiar with dimensions and how a billboard should look. Again, my only talent is writing.

I spent $900 in billboard advertising that month because that's what I budgeted. My book sales were higher than normal but it's impossible to know if it was from the billboards. I paused the billboards for a few weeks and my sales didn't drop so I knew the billboards had nothing to do with it.

I was almost done with my next book, *My Fox Ate My Report Card,* so I focused on that. It was a shame about the billboards, but I'd keep looking for alternative ways to advertise.

I checked my audiobook sales on ACX a few months later. I hadn't been keeping up with it because I'd forgotten about it. Since releasing it seven months earlier, it had gone from 50 sales a month to more than 200. I already knew that, but what I discovered that month made me freeze.

My bounties had increased by 700%. If you don't know, bounties are what you're paid by Audible when your audiobook is the first one a new subscriber buys. You don't get the bounty until the month after they are a member for 61 days. That bounty was $50 each at the time.

I immediately turned my billboards back on. It was unquestionable that drivers had responded to them and people who had never used Audible got my book from there before any other book.

I fidgeted with times, budget, and locations for the next few months so I could bring my spending down. I also tested billboards with a banner that displayed AVAILABLE ON AMAZON in some locations—those billboards proved to bring in more buyers than the billboards with my website name. After months of going through all the major cities, three at a time, I focused my billboards on Orlando and Los Angeles for the greatest returns. By early the next year, my bounties were up 3000% and I was spending a ton less.

If you're familiar with ACX, you know what happened in June 2019. ACX stopped paying bounties the same way for first books purchased.

They started giving direct referral links for us to give new subscribers, which they have to click on in order for you to get a bounty. Try as I might, I could not figure out a way to make that work with billboards.

While writing this book, I've placed a referral link to the audiobook on my website. I'm hitting myself in the head for not doing this sooner. I'll test this for at least three months before restarting billboards with my website banner (not Amazon) to lead customers there. The bounties aren't $50 anymore—they're $75 now.

In Oct 2018 I released *My Fox Ate My Report Card.* I left it with a cliffhanger that would not be resolved for more than a year. That wasn't my intention, but upcoming events kept me from completing it.

I had two interviews in November. One was by video about my writing career and focused on my advertising strategies. The other was a general website interview about my books. I believe this combination helped boost my sales for the holiday season.

I once heard that 33% of people you meet in life will like you. 33% won't like you. 34% won't care either way because they don't really know you. If you can cultivate relationships with that 34% then potentially 67% of people will like you. This is not an exact science but the theory of it holds a ton of potential for us as writers.

If you get a chance to be interviewed in a blog, vlog, or even a podcast you should do it. The more exposure you get the more chances you have to be seen by audiences that have never heard of you before.

I decided to create a hardcover version of *My Fox Ate My Homework* during this period. This completed a desire I had at the very beginning in 2016. I used to look at Amazon book sales pages and wonder how they got audiobooks and hardcovers to show there with paperbacks and eBooks. I thought it was amazing and made it my ultimate goal. I learned how later through the author Facebook groups.

I received another email from Heather at Disney Publishing Worldwide that same month (a year after the first one). I couldn't believe what she asked me.

She asked me to write the *Frozen 2 Junior Novelization.*

GOOD EXPERIENCE /
BAD EXPERIENCE

I spent the first seven months of 2019 working on the *Frozen 2 Junior Novelization*. It was an awesome learning experience in a different way to write. It was someone else's story (script), but I got to tell it in my own words and add scenes. I would describe it as a fun and unique experience.

The only downside was I completely immersed myself in the project. That's always a good thing, but it kept me from writing anything else until it was complete. My imagination was reserved until then for *Frozen 2*.

I created a series collection of the first three My Fox books in March. It didn't require me to be creative because all of the work was already done. I added the fourth book to the collection as a bonus to make it appealing. Readers would be paying the price of two books for four. This was done for both eBook and paperback.

The collection has done well, but at the same time, sales of *My Fox Ate My Cake* (book 2) and *My Fox Ate My Alarm* Clock (book 3) dropped drastically and have stayed that way. I suppose that's to be expected. I get $6 for this collection. If the same books are purchased individually, I get $11. But you have to keep in mind that only 30% of people who buy the first book buy the second one. Seventy percent of those buy the third one. The numbers go up to as high as 90% as the series progresses.

When I finished the My Fox collection, I tried to find a way to spend less time working on my advertising. I realized that once I was done with *Frozen 2*, I would be busy. I had been spending up to four hours a day fidgeting with Amazon and Facebook Advertising to keep them optimal. This was tough while working on one book, but I had two books in mind that I wanted to write, and I wanted them both out before Christmas. It would be nearly impossible because by the time I was done with *Frozen 2*, I'd only have four months to write and release the other two books.

I searched for someone to handle my advertising for the rest of the year and got a recommendation from a respected book marketer. He claimed to be getting a 300% return after expenses and his source was a professional at scaling it up. He only worked with big-name clients and got them huge returns over time. I thought that was great because at the time a

300% return was close to what I was getting.

I decided to use the professional based on the marketer's recommendation. The price was steep but would be worth it to maintain my sales while I focused on *Frozen 2* and later my other books. The price was $1300 a month plus all advertising costs. Yeah, it was hard to accept that, but I trusted the process.

The source blew through $700 on Amazon Advertising in the first week. There was no return on that. None. I suppose I could have been patient enough to see what happened the next week, but I was already out $2000 overall. I looked over the campaigns the source was managing and grew angry. Many of the keywords he had set up in the ads had more than 50 clicks and not a single order. It was obvious he was not managing them at all. The claim was he monitored it over four hours a day.

I decided to cut ties with this person and take my losses. He argued that it took months to make ads profitable (never said this up front). I knew that wasn't true because my ads were profitable from day one.

I'm only going to say this: don't let other people handle your advertising for you. This person put each keyword bid at seventy-five cents. Yes, that convinces Amazon to make many more impressions than if the bids had been twenty or thirty cents, but if not managed properly and there are a ton of clicks, money disappears quickly. That's great if a ton of sales are generated from those keywords but a nightmare if not.

After *Frozen 2* was done I got straight to work on the final My Fox book and released it in November. It was sobering to write because it was the end of writing about the boy (Joe) and Fox. I closed all the gaps that had been created since book one and even gave him superpowers (never shown in the previous books but always hinted at). It's probably my best work. I named it *My Fox, My Friend Forever*.

The other book I wrote is called *Epic Kids*, also released in November. I originally wanted to call it *Epic Kids from Outer Space* but figured that wouldn't be appealing to kids. *Epic Kids* reveals a transition for me from writing chapter books to writing middle grade novels. There are no illustrations in this kind of book. My focus had always been on reluctant readers, but this story allowed me to reach out to an older audience (up to 14). It's about an average kid who discovers he's a prince from another planet. I had a ton of fun writing it.

Frozen 2: The Deluxe Junior Novelization was also released in November.

By the way, I think the best books I write are the ones I have fun with. The ones I smile and laugh with. And the ones I cry with.

One last thing with advertising and reaching out to readers. It's well known in the marketing world that email is the most powerful tool we have. Based on that, it's suggested that authors have newsletters for readers (sent through email). This is done by collecting reader email addresses first, usually by giving away a free book or product from your website or the back of your book.

I tried this for six months. I think I got twelve subscribers and gave up on it.

The fact is I've sold 100,000 books without a newsletter. You don't have to have one. The question is would I have sold 200,000 books if I had a newsletter with active responders? I'm not sure, but I think it's a good idea for everyone to try it. Never eliminate tools unless they're broken.

SCHOOL VISITS

I had new challenges by the time January 2020 arrived. I had been contacted months before by a Boys & Girls Club and two schools with requests to make author visits. It was a tough decision for me to make because it went against a decision I made early in my children's author career.

Back in 2016, soon after I published *My Fox Ate My Homework*, I had planned to make as many author visits in schools as possible. This was because all of the research I had done online showed it was impossible to sell children's books without going into schools. As you know, this turned out not to be true for me.

Now that it was 2020, I decided to give it a shot. I had two posters printed on satin canvas and pasted to standing poster boards for *My Fox Ate My Homework* and *Epic Kids*. These were created at posterprintshop.com. I also had 500 bookmarks made at nextdayflyers.com. One side of each bookmark had information about *My Fox* and the other about *Epic Kids*. Both sides had my web address.

My first visit was at a Head Start in Perry, Florida with preschoolers, followed by a Boys & Girls club in

Mayo, FL that was the grantee for the Head Start. They had collectively pre-ordered 140 books. Zander and Regina came with me for these presentations. For the Head Start, I provided a coloring page for every child ahead of time with *My Little Fox*, the same book I brought to read to them (*My Little Fox Says Please*). Zander stayed by my side the whole time as I made the presentation and read. Regina stood to the side and talked with the teachers.

I made sure to include the kids as I read. With every scenario in the book ending in "My Little Fox Says Please," I finished each page by saying, "My Little Fox Says…" and they would shout, "Please!"

I ended the book and set it down then put on the same fox head from the costume I had worn at Zander's VPK class. The kids were sitting on the floor in an L pattern. I ran around the room my hands out for high fives and fists pumps, which they loved. I was done after making two laps, and Zander motioned for me to give him the fox head. I did; then he ran around the room the way I had, giving high fives and pumps. I thought the kids loved it when I ran around, but Zander was a rock star as the kids shouted and hollered in excitement for him.

That experience was exhilarating, and I was excited to head to the Boys & Girls Club. Things took a turn there though.

During this process I signed all 14o books. I set up the two posters at the Club. I figured my presentation there would be great because I had spent weeks memorizing a speech with lots of comedy to give.

When I spoke and waited for the laughs, I got blank stares. So I kept going and I kept getting blank stares. My speech was timed at forty minutes, but I cut it down to fifteen based on the responses. I was so flustered that I didn't think about reading passages from my books. I spent the rest of the time answering questions, which quickly turned into information about Zander's favorite video games and such. I felt bad because even my mom had traveled there to see the presentation.

I had to rethink things after I returned home. I tore up my speech and thought of ways I could turn things around. I'd be presenting to a school in Lake City, FL a week later and another school in Orlando, FL two weeks after that.

Here's what happened at those schools:

#1. For the kids in 5th and 6th grade – I confirmed they knew what an adverb was and further explained it. I advised that I try to eliminate as many adverbs from my books as possible to make the sentences stronger and that they should try to do the same thing with their writing. Then I told them that at their age I knew many of them had crushes on a boy or girl. This caused quite a commotion. I said they may be tempted to send their crush a love note or letter. More commotion. They may want their note to say, "I completely love you with my whole heart." The room blew up. I waited for the commotion to die down and advised they should eliminate the adverb to make the sentence stronger so it reads, "I love you with my whole heart." Tons more commotion.

#2. For the kids in 2nd – 4th grade – I stressed the importance of reading to become smarter but understood not everyone loves to read because they don't have time for it … there are video games to win. A little commotion. Sonic has to beat Dr. Robotnic. A little more commotion. Worlds have to be built in "Minecraft". Even more commotion. And you need as much time as possible to beat the bad guys in "Fortnite". The room blew up. After the commotion slowed, I said it was okay to play video games—even I do—but the more you read the smarter you get. The smarter you are the better you will be at video games (teachers liked this).

#3. Halfway through my presentations, I gave a confession: My name is not David Blaze. The rooms and auditoriums blew up in confusion. I explained that my middle name is David and my son's middle name is Blaze—David Blaze is a pen name; then I went further and explained my reasons for this.

#4. I explained that my love for writing started in the 5th grade when I wrote poetry for my classmates. It was silly poetry to make my classmates laugh, and it made me popular. I then gave the modern kids an example by picking one child and making a poem about them that I would have created back then.

In one auditorium I told the chosen girl I was going to make her famous and called her up on stage. Then I began to recite a predetermined poem that could easily be changed. *Note that this was insanely popular with 3rd graders and I made up ten poems for kids on the spot and only stopped because we ran out of time.

"My friend's name is Emily and she's super cool,
She never skips breakfast and she never skips school.
Her toes are green and her feet are blue,
If you don't believe me, make her take off her shoes.
Emily is a superhero with superpowers,
She can talk for days and read books for hours."

I then had all the kids clap and holler for the one I said the poem to.

One of the questions the kids asked me was, "What do you have to do to become a good writer?" I immediately said you have to read as many books as you can. The teachers loved this answer and one gave a "Hallelujah!" and asked me to repeat it.

I read three pages from two of my books at pivotal moments in the story. I stopped in the middle of both at a cliffhanger, put the book down and asked if they wanted to hear more. The answer was always a resounding yes.

All of these things were popular and won over the kids and teachers (though when I mentioned adverbs and crushes, one male teacher looked concerned, lol). For 1st – 5th grade I also gave out the bookmarks to all the kids.

I presold a few hundred copies. One school used a local bookstore for this. The Boys & Girls Club and Head Start bought copies directly from Amazon (140 of them!). Another school bought copies from me.

You really do have to be yourself and not a master robot with kids. Don't try to be funny unless it's natural—just like in regular conversation.

Kids are awesome and we can be too!

LITERARY AGENT
AND FINAL ADVICE

I took some time off to relax after the school visits. I jotted down some story ideas and honed my advertising like a guided missile. I was mentally worn out after completing all the projects in 2019 and had a hard time getting started with my writing again.

That was until a literary agent contacted me in April.

Mark was impressed with the success of *My Fox Ate My Homework* and called me to discuss writing a new book to present to publishers. I was excited to speak with him and we were on the phone for over an hour. My number one priority is self-publishing and I made that perfectly clear, but earlier in the year I had discussed being a hybrid author with another successful author.

I know what you're thinking. My very first experience in publishing was with a publisher and that didn't go so well. In fact, I did 13,999% better without one. What I didn't know back then was a shift was happening in the publishing world where authors were expected to do some or most of the marketing. I didn't do any marketing because I was naïve and unaware.

I signed a contract with Mark's agency and am working on the project we discussed. It's taking longer than expected because it's a form I've never written in before, even though I'm the one who suggested it. Mark loves the idea so I'm going to get it done.

That's what we do as authors, right? We get it done.

We also get distracted easily. Sometimes a million ideas hit us at once. I went from having no willpower to wanting to do six projects at once.

While working on the book for the agent, I:

- Published an eBook in April called *Gotta Catch the Easter Bunny*.
- Published an activity book in May called *My Fox and Friends Word Search*.
- Published the *My Fox Series books 5–6* eBook in May.
- Published the *My Fox Complete Series* eBook in May.
- Published an eBook in August called *My Skunk Goes to School*.
- And in September I'm publishing this book in

eBook and print.

So, yeah … I'm caught up for the year.

Well, it's been great talking with you, but I've got to go in just a minute. I've got a book for an agent to work on. Let's see … is there any last-minute advice I can give you?

* I'm a believer in the long tail of success with books. I've seen too many books have big launches and shoot up the charts but fizzle out within a month and sell next to nothing afterwards (this is for indie and mainstream). What good is having a bestseller if it's only a bestseller for a month or less? Sure, you could retain the title of best-selling author, but you wouldn't keep up the sales or profit.

* I'll tell friends and family what I'm writing but not give details about it. I wouldn't want to be in the middle of a story or scene and then have someone tell me that the book is a horrible idea. I don't want my enthusiasm to be swayed and killed off. Changes can easily be made after the book is done but not if I don't complete it because I believed someone who said it was no good.

* I write my chapter books and middle grade novels in Microsoft Word and use 14 point Adobe Garamond Pro font for paperbacks (12 point Georgia for eBooks), though I used 14 point Garamond on the earlier My Fox paperback books. The Adobe Garamond Pro is darker and more professional. My pages have been mostly black-and-white interior with white paper though I have a preference now for cream paper in middle grade novels. The My Fox trim sizes are 6x9 but my latest taste is 5.25x8.

* I always choose glossy covers instead of matte because I'm a sucker for shiny things. I don't like to pay more than $300 for covers. That's a price I found absurd in the early days and would have been a burden, if not impossible to pay. My first book covers didn't cost more than $12. I paid $1,200 for the *Epic Kids* cover because it was from a top talented artist, but that's way too much. I currently have a $50 premade cover for the paperback version, and it sells just as well as the $1,200 cover.

* I don't make my books returnable on IngramSpark anymore. I originally did and set a 55% discount since that's what bookstores want. At the end of 2018, after reviewing thousands of sales through them, I discovered an unacceptable return rate (large

orders likely from bookstores). I don't make books returnable now and the discount is not more than 35%. This allows them to be available to all online bookstores, including the biggest names. And yes, a school was still able to order books through an independent bookstore using Ingram.

I have a lot more to say, but it's time to work on that other book.

Be good. Keep writing. Publish your books. Do it all again.

CHLDREN'S BOOKS BY DAVID BLAZE

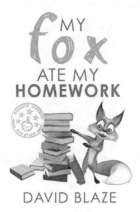

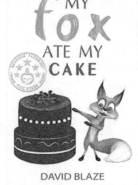

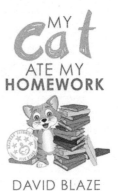

MY
fox
Begins

DAVID BLAZE

MY
fox
ATE MY
REPORT CARD

DAVID BLAZE

MY
fox
MY FRIEND
FOREVER

DAVID BLAZE

MY
little fox
SAYS PLEASE

DAVID BLAZE

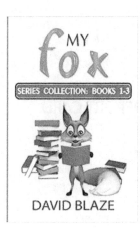

JANIE
GETS A GENIE
FOR CHRISTMAS

NORTH POLE

DAVID BLAZE

EPIC
KIDS

DAVID BLAZE

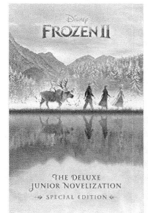

Disney
FROZEN II

THE DELUXE
JUNIOR NOVELIZATION
SPECIAL EDITION

GOTTA CATCH
THE EASTER BUNNY

DAVID BLAZE

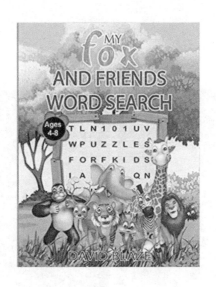

MY
Skunk
GOES TO
SCHOOL

DAVID BLAZE

About the Author

Timothy David and his son Zander Blaze live in Orlando, Florida with their crazy dog (Sapphire) and Zander's awesome mom! Timothy David loves to watch funny movies and eat pizza rolls! Zander Blaze loves to play video games and feast on chicken nuggets! Together, as David Blaze, they share lots of laughs and have lots of fun.....................

Wow! That's EPIC!

David Blaze

Made in United States
Orlando, FL
14 January 2024

42489152R00061